DATE DUE

10/23/96			
10/30/96			
6-30-03			

Demco

DISCRIMINATING EVIDENCE

Poems by

Mary Logue

First Book of Poetry Award

MID-LIST PRESS • DENVER

Copyright © 1990 Mary Logue.
All rights reserved.

Library of Congress Cataloging-in-Publication Data

Logue, Mary.
   Discriminating evidence : poems / by Mary Logue
      p. cm.
   "First book of poetry award"
   ISBN 0-922811-08-3 (cloth : alk. paper) : $16.95. — ISBN 0-922811-09-1 (pbk. : alk. paper) : $8.95
   I. Title.
PS3562.0456D5   1990
811'.54—dc20   90-39386
                                                                 CIP

For permission to use quotations we thank: Alfred A. Knopf, Inc. for the lines from the *Maltese Falcon* by Dashiell Hammett, © Dashiell Hammett; Simon and Schuster for the lines from *Attachments* by Judith Rossner, © Judith Rossner; Houghton Mifflin Co., for the lines from *The Long Goodbye* by Raymond Chandler, © 1953, Raymond Chandler, © renewed 1981 by Helga Greene, Executrix of the author. The quotation of Stéphane Mallarmé is from "Brise Marine" published in *Poésies* by Gallimard and translated from the French by Mary Logue.

The following poems have been published previously: "Watermelon in Florence," *Calyx;* "Father and Daughters" and "Sheriff," *Dacotah Territory;* "The Shadowing," *Fresh Air Magazine;* "Snow" and "Sweet Oranges," *Luna Tack;* "The Uncoupling," and "The Fish Are Drowning," *Scape*; "Field Notes," *Yellow Silk*; "An Answer to Sunstroke," *Gilt Edge;* "Unreturned Caresses," "Hitting Snow," "A Narrow Road," and "A Song in Killeshandra," *Milkweed Chronicle*; "Small Wish," *The James White Review*; and "A Ghazal," *Handbook of Poetic Forms.*

Manufactured in the USA

For Ruthmary and Robert Logue

"The flesh is sad, alas, and I've read all the books."
—Stéphane Mallarmé
"Brise Marine"

"I won't say goodbye. I said it to you when it meant something. I said it when it was sad and lonely and final."
—Raymond Chandler
The Long Goodbye

Contents

Unreturned Caresses	1
The Meaning of Words	3
The Shadowing	4
Mussels	6
Flowering Red	7
The Cheerio Kid	8
Responsibility	10
It's a Crime	11
Sailor's Holiday	12
Is This a Round Trip Ticket?	13
Father and Daughters	14
From Beyond	15
Pneumonia, 1960	16
Taos	17
Sheriff	19
Faster than the Eye	21
Cycle of Water	22
Field Notes	24
Snow	25
It's Like a Love Story	26
Small Wish	27
Missing You	29
The Last Letter	30
The Lost Dog	32
Courtroom	33

Anna	34
On the Move	36
The Hours	37
Hitting Snow	38
The Last Gift	39
Sweet Oranges	41
The Fish Are Drowning	43
Watermelon in Florence	44
No Princes	45
Thin Scars	47
Water	48
Given Life	49
Comfortable	50
Faith	51
Lilacs	52
The Uncoupling	53
What It All Adds Up To	54
First Snow	55
Incestuous Children	56
A Narrow Road	58
A Ghazal	60
An Answer to Sunstroke	61
Homesickness	62
How Big	63
Giving Thanks for the Turkey	64
A Song in Killeshandra	66

DISCRIMINATING EVIDENCE

UNRETURNED CARESSES

> "Now on the other side we've got what?
> All we've got is the fact that maybe
> you love me and maybe I love you."
> —Dashiell Hammett, *Maltese Falcon*

Internally, the murder was done,
as if a long-stemmed rose found
near the victim had worked its way
into her heart. During that moment,
her arms were wide flung and on her face
lingered the last rays of the sunset.
Nothing at the scene of the passion
indicated struggle.

To discover the murderer
I must fall in love with the victim,
her case entering the realm
of vengeance and unreturned caresses.
I visit her body at the morgue,
her eyelids fading to half moons,
her fingers trying to pull up the sheets
as the refrigerated cold sets in.
I mention the routine questioning
of the closest of kin and tell her
today the sky is in mourning and
I've never seen her more beautiful.

Delving through her rooms
I find pieces of her life
sticking to the mirror like lint.
Through a mesh of photos

Unreturned Caresses

her blonde curls fly like doves
over Lake Superior with her father
holding her up to the sky. He said,
"Her arms would come out of the dark for me."
In another shot she stands on the Golden Gate bridge,
hair grown dark as a thrush,
eyes searching the depth of the water.

Talking to her maid
the clues begin to add up:
"She kept no secrets and
I think she knew too much."
The woman next door stated
on the night of the murder
she heard loud groans
puncture the silence.

Living her life as if it were a game
of Clue got her into trouble.
As the mob moved in, she only laughed
at the dark-headed men with their eyes
in perpetual shade and blew them kisses.
The last line of her diary reads,
"Something I've long wanted
is almost within my grasp.
I can feel its pulse."

The reason for murder ran like electricity
between the two sides of the affair.
I see clearly now she chose
the explosion at the end of an embrace.

THE MEANING OF WORDS

There are words
that mean themselves.
Remember the night we sat
up in bed and whispered
them to each other.
I said: languid, cacophonous.
You said: multisyllabic, word.

The next day, on a fishing boat,
we felt tugs on our lines.
You pounded the gasping sea-
robin against the ship's hull
while I watched my fluke flop
over so only its vulnerable
white belly showed.

Now you have gone back to the city.
Night's languid air fills the rented
summer house. No words break
the silence, rather the soft whir
of a moth flirting with
a 45-watt bulb. I try not to think
what this means, but know

life could totter either way.
You are thinking of leaving me.
I can promise nothing. If we
stay together it might get
worse, but if we can say the
words that mean ourselves,
perhaps it will get better.

THE SHADOWING

Finally you leave for the office,
threading your way through the crowd
as innocent as a postman.
You're comfortable
that I'm home folding laundry
into easy messages for you,
but today I'm following a lead of my own.

Husband, you've gotten messy.
Working late and coming home
with a perfume on your skin that smells
like the inside of a bureau drawer.
I read notes on your wrist
when your arm hugs the pillow.
In the dark my body grows as large as a whale
and I beach myself, hoping you'll pull me
into the water. But you snore as though
you're on a deserted island.

I've taken a coat from the Goodwill,
clip-on sunglasses and a taxi
to the hotel opposite your office.
Holding my face against the glass
like a stray fingerprint, I pretend
that when you're gone I'll sneak in
and stab your secretary
on the damp spot below the hairline,
you know, where you used to kiss me
when you unzipped my dress.
The long spine of the needle would leave no mark,
and she would slump over the typewriter,

The Shadowing

stopped mid-sentence,
her mouth kissing the paper.
But this is as close as I'll get,
even if everything adds to my betrayal,
I will never get further than this hotel room,
a bed that offers itself to me
in the coldest way.

MUSSELS

I can't imagine the sea.
Growing up in the middle
of the country, I ate
frozen fish for years.
A trip to Belgium brings
small, flesh-colored creatures
to my lips. In a broth of wine,
celerys and onions they lie like
naked ladies, their boudoirs mercilessly
popped open to the world.
I say aloud, "They're the best
mussels I've ever eaten."
It's so hard to write about mussels
when they lie dead in fragrant sauce
and you know nothing about where they've come from
or why. Poets usually write about
the living, maybe the dead, but hardly ever
the eaten. And again to say the best
might be impossible—could it be only
that I was hungry, that the wine was good,
the company pleasant, the night crisp,
the room warm? What I can say for sure
is mussels were eaten in Brussels
on a late October night.

FLOWERING RED

I've straightened up the room
and will close the door on all traces of
your life wiped up and flushed away.
The .38 tore open your heart
and for a moment something bloomed
on your skin, a liquid flower
you held in your hands.

Pulling off a glove, I touch your hair
and wonder if it will grow into the pillow.

If only once you would have told me
where our love went, that small bird
that flew out from between us,
but you had to talk of the others
who protected you from the night.

The phone's off the hook.
If the *others* call you'll be busy
until finally busting down your door
they'll find you pale as an egg shell
under a sheet red as a hammer.
One question they'll want to ask,
but your emptiness won't answer,
only the .38 will shout! will shout!

THE CHEERIO KID

He needed all the doors in the house
left four inches open so any small
creature could roam through the rooms
at will. To himself he counted numbers
and thought of them as friends, but avoided
the black lagoon of his mother's eyes.

He lived on Cheerios in a blue bowl,
spooning in milk, sprinkling on sugar.
Hours it took to eat them, their
round open mouths sliding down his throat.
His father stood behind his over-sized
high chair and said his name. His name
was eaten by his father's voice.

There were too many doors and windows
in the world, too many arms and legs.
When he woke up in the morning, he knew
everything had changed immeasurably:
chairs pushed away from the table,
a letter lying opened on the piano bench.

Nothing could be counted on. When he forced
the calico cat down on the couch,
his mother twisted his ear and he couldn't
explain. He wanted the cat motionless,
caught in a square of sunlight where
each fiber of fur became a soldier
marching down its back.

The Cheerio Kid

He grew to be six foot three, shooting
as far off the ground as he could and
still he was no closer to heaven. But
one night, when he was deep in bed,
he glimpsed something hovering beyond
the last possible number, golden and
luminous, and he smiled, knowing it was
always there.

RESPONSIBILITY

for Mary

Your brown eyes tremble
as I sit across from you drinking coffee.
You're confused by this thing called *love*.
If only we were five;
ribbons tying back our hair,
mine curlier than weeds,
yours black and straight as a stick.
But we're in a fancy cafe and someone
wants you to stop reading books
as if your life depended on it.

In the spring the snow melts and so do our hearts.
We're a little older, far from the girls
the boys kissed in the dark corners of school.
I watch you purse your lips and sigh.
I wish I could promise you we'd never grow up,
promise you that the baby you fear you carry
is made of plastic and can only cry tap water tears.

IT'S A CRIME

From behind Levelor shades I peer out,
my eyes in darkness, my mouth in light,
and smile faintly, the sun resting like a match on my lips.
When I look down there are bars painted
across the bed we slept in.

Before the sun was up, you stole away.
The door's whisper woke me and I ran to the window.
In the street you lit a cigarette, cupping the flame
close to your mouth as if it were sacred.
I watched until your back turned into another shadow.

And so our meetings end: you walk into the day
and I return to bed to smell the odor of what
passed between us. *When will I see you again?*
The question dies as quick as a victim who only
feels the knife when it is pulled out of the body.

My friends tell me to stop seeing you,
but there can be no interrogation of our love
for it is the biggest lie of all and
two wrongs make a right as we meet
in a darkness that hides all shadows.

SAILOR'S HOLIDAY

What notes a guitar can play
when the hand that strums it
belongs to a sea-muscled sailor.
The waitress lolls on the bed
and watches the tattooed eagle
soar toward her.

Salt she licks the length of his neck
and thinks of fish. When his
comes squirming into her,
they begin the rocking of land
bound waves. They only just met
that night. The tray she carried
high held many mugs of beer,
but he grabbed her around the waist
and sent the beer sailing.
Foam on the white-starched
uniform and the eagle's wings.
Now, watching his bottom-blue eyes
roll back, she points her toes
for her own perfect dive.

Just as they fall asleep
he whispers her a promise.
Only a bottle set adrift
on the widest sea. No one
will ever scoop it up and
no one will ever answer.

IS THIS A ROUND TRIP TICKET?

The breaking up of winter is a secret
given away in the bark of trees
and the new song the wind sings.
I know a slender secret:
truth has many sides.

On the phone, I tell a friend
that my job keeps me going,
my home is well heated, and my bed
dressed with clean sheets.
I tell no lies. But when I find
my coffee grown cold, I pour it
into the sink with the regret
of a hundred nights alone.
People have been subtracting
themselves from my life.
Some by moving to a small town
in upstate New York, while others
board planes that never land.

We all have heard the sentence
handed down before we were even born,
the penalty for our first breath,
but we go on, smiling, saying all is well,
even as the ranks are broke on
either side, we keep walking forward
down the street, until it, too,
drops away below our feet and
we are left hanging, kicking at the air.

FATHER AND DAUGHTERS

Father, sometimes I think 3M has locked you up,
given us a photocopy, and you are working late into the night.
Small digits replace stars as you total the universe
on your pocket calculator.

It must be hard to have only daughters
and one a poet and one a painter
and one a drinker and one, still young,
unsure how she will be as good as a son to you.

As a child, I heard you say, "I know everything,"
and believed you.
And still that belief rises up in me
like a flock of blackbirds over a field.
When my car breaks down or my lover
leaves me, I think you know it
and can fix it, that you steal in at night
to be sure air is moving in and out
of my body, that I am watched over.

You have grown thinner, Father,
wearing down to that inner
landscape of bones that
has held up your skin for so long.

Maybe the photocopy is only in my eyes,
the picture I carry sheathed in plastic so it won't yellow.
It's time to tear up the picture,
time to wake up from my guarded sleep
and look at you as a man,
not only a father, but a man with daughters,
the stars in his sky.

FROM BEYOND

From beyond death, I look back at the slit
I've squeezed through. Incredible!
The moments I remember are next to me
stored in water like red agates.
Above me the sun has turned
into the black eye of a cat, winking on and off at will,
I'm not sure whose.

Moss is growing over my face,
while a snail slides down my backbone, sound
comes like waves, only voices of the past,
my father calling me to wake, or a lover
urging me to let go, break away from the world.

I've broken away. I'm alone.
My stomach empty. The carpet pulled out from under me.
Not a soul in sight and I'm fearless
in a whole new way. No more sleepless nights,
no more wishing the impossible,
I've reached the end of my rope and gone beyond.

I miss you, the smell of your skin.
But all I can tell you is the last breath
tastes the same as the first.

PNEUMONIA, 1960

Back against a cold wall,
feet braced on the linoleum,
the child sits at the end of the hall.
Behind a closed door
her parents are watching TV.
Past midnight she woke when her bed
filled with balloon people.

Now her eyes are drops
that yearn to fall,
but she props them open.
Afraid the night will close
in on her she fights sleep,
punching the air with her fists.

When she lies down
the bedclothes foam around her face
and she feels she is drowning in her own sea.
She concentrates on breathing,
but sometimes it slips away,
just as a dream dissolves
when it's within grasp.

If she thought her parents could help
she would call out to tell them
of the wind that lives near her mouth,
stealing the air from her body.

TAOS

Like rubbing a silver *milagro*,
or pressing my eyes hard in the dark,
like breaking turkey bones,
or catching the hiss of a star
as it tumbles through the sky,
I wish to go back to Taos.

Think of cilantro and adobe,
a bridge over a black ravine
and the hot spring you bathed in.
How your smooth body arced in water.
You yelped as I took
your picture with my brownie camera.

We registered at a hotel
that had a courtyard and opened
our window wide to let in
all the fine dust of the town.
A bed with a mattress higher
than my waist stood in
the middle of our room
and I jumped on it naked
and you took my picture.
We made slow love and ate
bean enchiladas in the perfect
order of sustenance.

Now I have two pictures:
a woman bathed in sunlight,
a man dipped in spring water.
What happened between them

Taos

was light shearing across water,
a woman bouncing off a bed
and a man always catching her.

I'm not sad that half a country
divides us and another half
must be driven to reach Taos,
but in the way that I try
to part the past like a heavy
curtain and walk back into
the white-walled room,
I want to go back to Taos.

SHERIFF

My uncle is a sheriff in spirit,
in legend a drinker, a tale-teller.
His birth was royal:
half man, half animal.
For eyes he has two guns.

Now, leaving the mountains,
his horse is tired and lame
with sage growing in its tail.
My uncle lies across the saddle.
He has counted the horse's steps for weeks.
With every step, a bone has broken.
He hangs in the saddle,
a gunny sack of a man.

Sheriff,
the buffalos are gone.
You rattle when you laugh,
shaking the blank dice of your bones.
Your hat has fallen off,
a pile of decaying straw.
Your tin star has gone back to the sky.

The mountains are laughing,
their eyes red with deer meat.
The air is filled with the noise
of pine trees snapping in the wind.
The sheriff groans at the sound
and falls through layers of earth,
horse manure, Indian hair,
gnawing teeth, and a buffalo mane.

Sheriff

The stable door blows open.
The horse heads straight for the oat pail.
A woman gathers up my uncle.
She strips him and lays him in the straw.
She bathes him and puts flowers in his hair.
She cuts off her hair and wraps him in it.
She takes a step, and holds out her hand
to show him the way.

FASTER THAN THE EYE

A stillness and the glow inside the room
were all that woke me, the bed cleared off
like a lake swept by the morning sun.
You were still drowning in sleep
and I watched your easy breath before
rescuing you from the sheets.

You've come from quiet people,
growing into marriage and out again.
Wandering around your apartment,
sometimes you will stop dead center
and wonder where you are, staring
at the sheets of paper you hold.
A letter from me will not solve
any of this but I write to tell you
of that morning and the sun.

The lake is all around us,
we are in it and laughing as
the waves rush to see the magic
that swims between us like
fish darting faster
than the eye can see.

CYCLE OF WATER

for Helen (1954-79)

It rains in the darkest city.
I try to write. The words are heavy
as rocks the farmers leave
in the field and plow around.
One wriggling vein curves up
my thigh and I feel old.
You will never grow old.

The rain falls from a blank sky,
forming around the building tops.
Lightning is feebly flashing.
It's a day that takes twice
as long to wander through.
I want *things* to be fair, but
all's fair in death and rain.

The rain here splats off
the sidewalk so an umbrella
is little protection.
Mine fills with wind.
If you were carrying one
next to me, we would walk close,
spokes bumping, to talk of men
and work and how old we should be
to have our first child.
How that age rose as we grew,
always floating two years
above our heads.

Cycle of Water

When I miss you,
I don't know
what I'm missing.
I would miss the rain:
cycle of water softening
the city, slick streets,
slipping through the air,
something is leaving,
something is gone,
and so I miss you, sister.

FIELD NOTES

When we met at the bar you told me
your woman had left you,
a typed note the only explanation.
I bought you a beer but that wasn't
enough. So we slept together, old lover,
like two hunters after the same prey.
We saw it slither out between us.

During the night, you plunged into your jungle.
I stayed behind in a warm glade.
Thick veins coiled around me.
I stood motionless, watching
like I watched my parents kiss
when they thought they were safe.

I'm jotting down field notes,
staring at men's faces while they sleep,
their pale eyelids closed over the moving eye.
I take their temperatures by holding
my finger in their breath. I probe
this palpitating thing we call love,
or heart, or rub of skin against skin.
I want to know how it grows
between people, warm and lush,
orchid of love, and how it fades away.

SNOW

The woman stares out the window to watch the snow
in the gray morning, moving into day.
Too late she stays, but feels the urge to go.

The snow is ashen petals, opening slow,
flowers that tell winter is here to stay.
The woman stares out the window to watch the snow.

Somehow, she thought he'd have the grace to know
words weighted with love were not for play.
Too late she stays, but feels the urge to go.

A part of her is cold and white, and so
in bed, the man had had his way.
The woman stares out the window to watch the snow.

The sheets are white, cold, and seem to glow.
Her clothes in piles are near to where they lay.
Too late she stays, but feels the urge to go.

His footsteps sound behind her, moving slow.
He's sad, not knowing what to say.
The woman stares out the window to watch the snow.
Too late she stays, but feels the urge to go.

IT'S LIKE A LOVE STORY

It's like the end of a love story
when they still love each other
but they are leaving anyway.
Trying to turn the pages of the book so fast
that they tear them out of the binding.

It's like that
sometimes there's no explanation.
You are kissing your lover and he turns into a salesman.
You feel like a public building.
Later when you're lying in bed
the whole state of Montana is spread out on the sheets
between his dreaming body and yours.
You know this could be either the beginning or the end.

It's like the beginning of a love story.
They don't know why they've come together.
She's met men who have deeper set eyes,
he's met women who haven't talked as much.
The lights go out.
They're in each other's arms.

SMALL WISH

>for James L. White (1936-81)

>> We poets crave immortality.
>> —Breaker Morant

In late February all we had was
still air and sour snow.
You were only 45 and your heart
was a balloon blown up to burst.
Traitor, you called it.
When we went to the movies
you fell in love with
Breaker Morant.
Handsome and healthy,
his heart was a thundering
hammer in his chest.
When he was blown off
his wooden chair by the force
of a dozen bullets,
we touched fingers and cried.
I saw the movie again,
my fingers touching a letter
that told of your death.

A parent lives on in the seed,
that bead of immortality.
You sowed words corn-like in
their luminosity,
and as I grow old,
I hope to pass them on.
You knew ecstasy and submission,

Small Wish

slight bird and cracked sidewalk,
whine of winter and the white
landscape of bed sheet.

After the movie, we drove home
through hushed snow
and were as silent.
Touching the windshield's hoarfrost,
you said it was almost warm,
then you said,
"I want to live forever."

MISSING YOU

Missing you is a walk down a road with
darkness at the end holding out its winding arms,
and I shrink and turn in bed thinking that
only because there's not enough room for you
are you not in it, why else would you be
so many miles away from me in the middle
of the night when a single pane is all
that keeps the stars from falling in on me,
those white periods that have stopped
no known sentences, noiseless, noiseless,
they fall as perfect dew and sleep
is further away than you are and I still
want you more than I've ever told you.

THE LAST LETTER

Husband, as I write this
from the porch I can see the water
is clear with no wrinkles on it.

Since you've left, the world, thin and flat,
is a record I play over and over.
Watered-down shadows lay under the trees
in the field you plowed last spring.
Stopping near them, I look at the lines in my hand
which tell me no stories.

Old Dog, lying on the front steps, growls in his sleep.
I sit down next to him and watch
as the day burns down like a candle.

In this weather, I feel
a gnawing in my bones as ice forms.
One of the picture windows shattered late last night.
When I went to look all I saw was myself
caught in the slivers of the glass on the floor.

Then I wished you were upstairs.
Your mouth made my tits well up
like buds breaking open in spring.
Even when you kicked me the bruise
glowed blue like the middle of a fire.
Remember the way the pond looked at sunset,
calm like no one ever walked on it?
But you claimed the winds died down for
scientific reasons.

The Last Letter

I can't forget your back bobbing up
and down the dirt road.
You never felt the stone I threw,
it didn't make it past the gate,
or heard the shout I yelled as
you slunk over the hill and
I know you'll never get
this letter.

THE LOST DOG

    for Robin

When I knew the dog
was really gone, when we
stood in the woods, early spring,
before buds, and you called
his name, not mournfully,
more angry that something
you loved could leave you,
I wanted to hear the dead leaves move.

There's so little we, any of us
humans or dogs,
can give each other. A little
warmth at the end of a long cold
day, some water, or even that
moment of being together,
the clouds lifting off the
sky to show us a land of
billowing, swirling masses of white,
and we stood quiet, then
walked back through the trees
calling.

He ran away from home
looking for you and now you spend
your days in search, and even nights,
wake up at three and go for walks
along the lake, the water carrying your voice,
a gift to sleeping people who turn softly
and reach out for someone else.

COURTROOM

In the courtroom people are scattered
over the benches. No one sits too close.

The judge and public defenders are dressed
in the dark uniforms of decision. You wear
a white sweater dirty from sleeping
on the jail cots. Outside it is raining.

You are on trial for the men who have touched you:
Harold, the businessman from Detroit,
who wanted you so badly, he came
while you were still in the bathroom.
Skinny Will from Omaha didn't want to be touched
instead laid you out like silk fabric and stroked you.
Or Lenny, who sliced your ear with his knife
to show you he wasn't afraid of blood.

The man behind all these men is not around.
Once on a train he broke down and said he loved you,
then went to con the businessmen in the next car,
while you sat still, watching the telephone poles slide away.

The last time you saw him he was sleeping on his side.
You left the joint where he could find it for breakfast
and the memory of his body, shiny as a piece of raw liver,
hurts you still.

ANNA

If she had lived in New York
she would have jumped
in front of a subway train,
no matter what, no matter
where, the end would have come
to dear Anna as she asked it
to come, roaring over her
in a crowd of people.

For she had discovered
a horrible thing as
she sat alone in her room,
thinking of what dress
she would wear that night,
of how she would pile her hair
cascading down her shoulder,
oh and her shoulder would gleam
powder and lotion and perfume
would waft from her as
she went down to dinner.
She could distract herself,
but the eyes she was seeing
through were Vronsky's and
then his thoughts would come
and she would know he still
admired her, still loved her,
still wanted her, but it had all
dulled and no matter how she
rubbed at their vessel of love
it would never shine again,
never be as it was

Anna

the first time she saw him,
his shoulders rising out of
a swirl of furs and coats,
the engine's furious smoke
and the sound of something
stronger than anything
she had ever known roaring up
and sweeping over her.

ON THE MOVE

You're on the move. The land's at rest. The car lights
shine on whatever is available, Shell stations, the largest

cross in the world, white plaster against the night sky,
houses grown together like toes in a shoe.

You're young yet. The first woman you loved
married a mechanic in Arizona, the second

has two kids on welfare. But that was years ago.
You don't love anyone now, instead you're searching

for less, scanning whatever's available. Late at night
when the trucks rumble by on the freeway you kiss

a woman's shoulder and it feels like you're learning something.
You're traveling to the country's end. After two days drive

L.A. glows on the horizon, the freeway thick with cars,
a human river rushing to the water's edge. You're tired

and let the car roll to a stop on the beach.
Love *must* be the answer you think as you watch

the stars, further out at sea, still driving away.

THE HOURS

The hours will sound all around us.
Nothing dies, but simply turns its back
on hands flapping in the wind.

Tell me things I can't believe.
As the day ends, I will believe them,
the sun slipping into the horizon.

Without trying to strangle anything
the water flows down the narrow river,
pulling the banks in behind it like a zipper.

Everything is closing down.
The streets are emptier than a lawn chair at dusk,
the house is silent

waiting to be lit,
and you sit wishing for the bed to be
a sea you could sail away on.

I want to believe
the space between us can collapse
with your arms forming a clock around me.

Days will stand on end like sunflowers.
The hours will sound all around us.

HITTING SNOW

Through the night the dog whimpers.
When I look out back he blends into the snow
but his cries pierce me like a child's
fingernail whittled down to a nub of pain.

As the puzzle of night is pulled apart,
an Indian couple break a window
to get into their apartment below me.

I imagine the woman downstairs,
her long black hair a curtain
she waits for him to part.
But he pounds boards over the window,
then with that movement still in his arms
he pushes her down on the bed.
He feels he's hitting snow
as his blows don't stop
but sink into whiteness.

The dog is silent
listening to the woman cry.
I pull the pillow over my head
and pray for a weather to cover us all.

THE LAST GIFT

    for Kate

What we imagine is so simple—
a door opening, the air
parting before her hands,
while her body, unattended,
crumpled like a cloth.

We hope she joined those who
glide over snow. They wonder when
we fall and laugh as field after
field of white unfold before their eyes
like the petals of a water lily
blossoming in the sun.

They swim in water
we have yet to know.

Don't call her back. Don't detain her.
With the last gift of your heart, let her go.

There are no instructions for those left behind.
We touch hands in the half darkness,
and a flicker of light passes between us.
Silence walks into the room like another person.
The dogs don't bark.
The children hug our legs.

The Last Gift

Outside, throwing bales of hay over a fence,
a dark-haired girl calls in the horses.
They nudge against her legs like
snow blowing in from the north.
Combing their manes and whispering in their ears, she is
unafraid of the darkness that grows around her.

SWEET ORANGES

    for Yasunari Kawabata

Feet folded under her,
the woman sits quietly on the floor.
In her downcast eyes,
the straw mat is a map of a foreign country
in which she is trying to find her way.
If only she could take off her slippers
and place a wet rag
against her rice-floured face,
but she doesn't dare stir,
afraid of being caught
in an ungraceful moment.

Soon a businessman from Tokyo will come.
She will feed him sashimi
and at the end of the meal,
sweet oranges cut like lips on a plate.
If he insists, she is only to wet
her mouth with saki.
Then, if it pleases him,
play music to cut through the night
like a silken cord.
She will start nothing
but wait for his hands
to find the nape of her neck,
the sole of her foot, the places
where her skin has never felt pressure.

Sweet Oranges

She calms her mind until
it is a white plain with no trees
but a bear comes lumbering up over the horizon,
his mouth blazing as if he has caught the sun.

Footsteps sound in the hallway.
The paper screen moves back.
She stands up like a white stork
about to take flight
for that country which is within herself.

THE FISH ARE DROWNING

I glance up at her in the kitchen,
her back is as broad as a cupped hand.
"It says it's going to go below zero tonight.
It's here in the paper."
She doesn't stop chopping up onions for stew.
The cutting board is worn thin in the middle.
I can't see her face.
I know she wants me back in her bed.
What can I tell her I've found on the couch?
It all started with winter.
Her body became a pond, icing over.
There was no way for me to get in.
Even the fish are drowning.

WATERMELON IN FLORENCE

Mother, what we love is watermelon.
We find it everyday near the end of the market.
Green-spotted, it rolls out of the ice
like a sea lion. The smiling man cuts us
generous slices. And we try on shoes.
Each of us has bought two pair. You
would think us happy if you saw us.
Three American girls walking in new
shoes and eating red chunks from the middle
of the melon. Men do follow us.
Dodie wishes she didn't have blonde hair.
The weather hangs heavy, 90° since
we've arrived. Last night the shrunken
grandmother at the *pensione* yelled
at us for coming in late,
but in Italian. I can only
wish her *buon giorno* so I couldn't
explain that if the windows
were left open the mosquitos swarmed
in like our worst worries and if
closed we couldn't breathe and sank
in sweat on our cots. Robin looks
like a madonna. It's the line of
her shoulders. I watch her standing
on a corner in this foreign city
and she seems to carry a child
in her arms. We miss you and
have talked of the silver swivel
rack that your shoes twirl around on.
The night comes over the river in Florence.
There are many things I could write of
but you know watermelon. Even here
it tastes the same and is cooling
to the forehead like a mother's kiss.

NO PRINCES

    for Amy

Like a deflated body,
the red cloth sprawls across the table.
Each stitch you sew pulls it
together in a life of its own.
It's night on Hennepin Avenue.
From the White Castle under your window
issue no princes. That's another story
with an ending far sweeter than you could stand.
You sit and watch the breeze dance
your clothes off their hangers.
I sit and watch you.

Two months ago you opened
your lover's door and found
him in the tub, rubbing
another woman's shoulders,
you backed out into the hall ready
to learn a new dance.
One where no one followed,
yet the steps led somewhere.
Dressed in pink, you were no piece of candy
and the night undid its wrapper at your feet.

Tonight we go to a gay bar.
Leaning on the counter, we watch
the princes strut around us.
We wear our femaleness like a ratty fur
and click glasses. Still for a second,
glasses uplifted, the music

No Princes

beats out the night. It lasts
long on Hennepin Avenue,
we won't go home 'til dawn covers
the streets like a red cloth.

THIN SCARS

A hot stalking summer night,
the stars are small fires of distant tribes.
Heat lightning tears across the sky, warning us.

On a hospital bed a woman lies,
her face waxen as an old doll,
battle plans drawn on her body.

Sitting in the empty chairs around us
are the hours we have waited.
I think of escaping into the night
where the streets are empty arteries.

Instead I stay across from my father,
watching him pop pills like prayer beads,
talking of weddings and birthdays as if they could
help him understand what is happening.

When she is rolled past us, still breathing,
the night becomes the night again:
no longer an end but a procession
and we march out into it feeling

the thin scars that run through our lives
like streaks of lightning
etched across the sky.

WATER

> Water has the quality of forgiveness.

Swimming, the dark nights with you return.
We sailed through seaweed and slender fish,
our eyes closed, our breath breaking
our hearts and through the water came
tiny bubbles tearing open lungs.
I felt as empty as a dried shell
when your body floated away in the tide.

There are long reaches of the night
that must be entered alone, the clean-swept rooms,
empty parking lots, and white beaches of sand.
Walking, I hear only the waves slapping the shore
but your name pounds in me like a heart beat.
To enter the water a whole person takes time.
I leave a pile of unshed tears with my clothes.

In five years we will meet on the shore of Guatemala.
You, wearing a straw hat as protection from the sun,
will walk up behind me, sitting on a rock, counting
the waves as they leave the shore. When I turn
you will notice the wrinkles around my eyes,
the crevices water makes as it rushes out to sea.

GIVEN LIFE

There's a life I want to lead
but the hollow in my chest is too large.
Fear glides through my veins, dispersing,
gleaming and white, bubbles of air like
irritating pearls which explode
when they reach the heart. If only

I could wake up each morning with thoughts
as pure as a saint's and as fixed, but where
there is no passion, there is no life.

Often, I leave my lover to sleep alone.
Car lights wash my windows and
the rain falls on the bending sycamores.
The smell of marigolds is bitter in the air.
No one can protect me from these moments.
When I sleep, I dream of the night ending
and wake more puzzled than ever.

I've begun to watch my mother.
She sits at the kitchen counter,
drinking tea with lemon as she does the crossword puzzle.
For what she's given up, she's received this world:
the words contained in squares, the cardinal
in her muted colors opening a seed,
and her daughter on the phone, asking,
Mom, do you ever want to be young?
I can't tell her I'm afraid, but she knows.
The life she's given me is her only gift.

COMFORTABLE

My father and I are driving through
a field of snow and it is snowing.
No horizon between land and sky.
Only a cottonwood tree stands out,
its dark branches sifting
the snow. I want to say
how beautiful it is
but I only stare out the window.

We're not saying much in the car.
He's smoking a cigarette. I am
his daughter and a grown woman.
The wind isn't blowing
and the snow comes straight down.
The cottonwood just stands there
in the white and silent land.
He doesn't say he loves me but
like the snow it comes straight down,
it falls straight down on me.

FAITH

Every Sunday morning is the same.
Her father drinks coffee.
She spreads the newspaper at his feet.
Only this Sunday Jesus stares back
from the front page, the Story of the Shroud.
She reads it as if it were scripture.
Her father folds his hands in his lap.

It makes sense to her:
a light bulb burst inside his body and,
like a heart pounding out its blood,
soaked the linen cloth with light.
Everything is a simple matter of faith.
For her, the birds flying across the sky
are the check marks of another good year
and the stars are held up in some eternal embrace.
Even when she pricks herself sewing, she sees
the blood as a holy river running through her body.
She tapes the picture of Jesus to her mirror
under her favorite rock star.

That night she kneels at the foot of her bed,
Mother, someday I'll be a nun.
Her rich black hair covers her shoulders.
As her mother pulls up the sheets
a glow reflects off the young pure body.

LILACS

The lilacs are too sweet;
it isn't their fault.
I smell them, leaving
the darkness of the late movie.
Night is falling,
scattering its black pods through the air.

A few old men still line the avenue,
spitting on the sidewalk.
I cross the street to avoid them.
The lights rise up on their slender stalks.

Sometimes, life hands out these small endings,
these lyrical notes out of tune,
and the day gives up its light
like a dog shaking off moisture.

The only place I have to go is home,
and I walk slowly, taking with me
the last embers of light on a faded screen,
and the lilac smell, the cheap perfume
all women wear in spring.

THE UNCOUPLING

> That they'd been born to a condition
> I'd spent my life trying to achieve.
> —Judith Rossner, *Attachments*

I always slept with my sister's arms around me.
Attached to my side, her body was a flesh cocoon.
Our breasts lay next to each other
as easily as eggs in a paper carton.
When we walked down the street
people stared, trying to understand
what held us together.
We were connected in a way that lovers envied,
but the doctors decided to separate us.

On two rolling tables we were pushed
into the operating rooms, our last sleep together.
The doctors fingered our skin
as if it were tissue paper
and told us we wouldn't feel a thing.

Now, I hold a man in my arms at night.
After making love, I stare at him
and the sheets tangled around our bodies.
Hoping it will tell me something
I touch the red scar
that colors my side like another mouth.
It is as quiet as the man resting beside me.
He has entered me in every possible way
and pushed me to a point
where I am truly alone.

WHAT IT ALL ADDS UP TO

If memories are pumpkin seeds
they're meant to be shelled and sucked on,
or if beads, they're rustled through fingers,
hoping to add up to wisdom and time.
Remember the hush descending before
the tornado pulls the roof off
your grandfather's house. A pipe
sticks out from the old man's mouth, percolating.
He has brewed a long time. Touch
your mother's face shining with the
warmth of a new laid egg. Your brother and sister
tie the laces of their shoes together.
You stand on one leg dreaming of the day
you bought the dog from the pound:
eager hound faces, tongues leaping
from their mouths. The pipe clicks
on the cellar floor like a light
switch turned off and when you look
at your grandfather's face you know
he's thinking of blowing skirts and heather fields.
There are memories that bust open
fuller than the shell that contained them,
that count for more than the time
they passed through. A face held
gentle in the mind can be studied
night after night when the air
is sweet with the loss of the sun.
Grandfather's face was potent and
you saw his eyes ripen to the breaking
of berries, fresh from the brambly
bush, and you remember the roof
lifting off, a shout, and you ran
from the cellar to find
the dog huddled in hay.

FIRST SNOW

Now, when the sun goes down at four
there are no consolations - I once
had the hope that the falling night
would pull down powder curtains but
Manhattan streets eat snow
before it knows the ground.

You know none of this. Boiling buckets
of corn after church are what you remember,
and trees full of green fruits, avocado, lime.
In the other room, you turn on the television
while I keep my face close to the darkening window.

I wonder if you wish for anything as I yearn
for snow: the underside of small objects,
where white springs out of black dusting pine
boughs, a pumice to soften spiny needles.
I see again the crystalline-lashed trees,
remember the cat bristling at the burn,
ice on the pond so thick the fish drowned,
back when the first skiff of snow was all
a northern child could imagine of heaven
and stars and wings and those frozen
tears of the dead people I'd never see.
The flannel sheet of whiteness made
the roads reverse blackboards. I'd write
huge messages to anyone looking down on me.

INCESTUOUS CHILDREN

for Jamie (1955-71)

When you were four
and I was seven,
we would sleep together.
I told you stories
of children lost in the woods
who survived by eating berries.

When we woke up in the morning
you were on my side of the bed
I was on yours.
We had rolled over each
other in the night,
dreaming of waves.

Now when people ask me
what you looked like,
it's easy to say you had
red hair and blue eyes.
They're satisfied.
Who could understand
from words alone that
your hair lived the royal
life of curls and sways
and that your eyes were
the color of water over
white sand, the blue
leaching through like
a school of minnows.

Incestuous Children

There have been red-haired men
I've loved, taken to bed,
held in my arms, staring
into their eyes until they've
blinked me away. Do I think
someday a wallet will open
and show me a picture
of you cutting timber
in Northern Minnesota,
a rough beard sheltering
your mouth like a heavy hand?

I've never faced a harder truth
than death telling me
only sleep can bring you back.

It's late and I'm so tired
writing you this that
my hands want to leave
the end of my arms and
curl up like cats
on a woven rug.

I know sleep is the red-haired
lover I'll never find tonight.
He says my bed is too narrow,
my bones stick out,
and he hates the dreams
that fill the bed
like incestuous children.

A NARROW ROAD

There's a road
with only enough room
for one car. If you meet
another you must stop,
get out, and discuss
who saw the last
wide spot. On this small
road is a church with
a graveyard, the bones
in some quarters
piled up of families
on families.
The others left this
country of peat
fires and oiled wool
and sweet music when
the potatoes turned black
as they were pulled
from the ground,
and the good food
was shipped to
England. They went
on creaking ships,
coffin ships, they
crammed on and hoped.
And they dreamed of
clouds of deep cream,
beds of down, and
grandchildren,

A Narrow Road

who would have children,
who would someday
drive down the narrow
roads of a green, green
country to find out
what had been
left behind.

A GHAZAL

There's an inside of me and an outside of me.
The clouds block the sky and the grass has dried golden.

Only a fool would try to love when the heart's in the wrong place.
The tree is trying to tell me something but I'm deaf with longing.

Take away my pen, my paper, the table, and I am only
a woman, crouched over the air, thinking.

My bed sags in the middle and my dreams get caught in my throat.
The wind comes in my window but the stars are stuck on the screen.

It doesn't take very long to realize you're dead, but alive,
you can go minutes without knowing it. Take a deep breath.

AN ANSWER TO SUNSTROKE

Heat bounces off the white refrigerator
and around me, the room caves in on itself.
Trapped in a summer day with no door in sight
I begin to expose myself.
The *you* I write about is you.
I won't write anymore until you answer.

Too hard to talk,
instead I swim through these days.
No love getting in the way of sleep.
Nothing feels better than white sheets.

Unable to draw a picture of what I want
I think it doesn't exist.

Every night the moon travels farther from the earth.
No one has noticed but me.
With the window ledge sturdy under my elbows,
I watch the stars fall from the sky
and hold my secrets close like children.

Looking ahead,
the road is an arm stretching out to touch me,
behind are only mirages of heat.

HOMESICKNESS

The trees here are good trees,
linking earth and sky as they should do.
Night laps at the shore of the buildings
as I walk down the Quai des Briques
staring in windows of restaurants,
at frites and steak. There is beauty
here, but it stays outside of me.
Cobblestone streets change names
from block to block. I name what is
missing: trees, air, water. They are
here in Brussels, but different and in
this difference I'm lost. Take the trees.
They are tall, grow leaves, but the bark
pulls away from the trunk. They're
dappled without any light, as if a disease
is part of them. I know they are
healthy but in my heart, I am sick.
It is a small sickness, a weightless feeling
as I turn corners that reveal nothing
I have ever seen before. I check
the mailbox, I watch the phone.
I think home, home. It's a soap, an
ointment. It's where I know how
to breathe. There the trees hug
their bark around them like fur
in winter. Snow on the ground.

HOW BIG

Sitting, drinking coffee with three women, we decide
that women don't write about big enough things,
they write too much about the small details, the things they

know, the lives they lead, and we decide
to write about the larger issues, about
the things we don't know, can only imagine.

So I think about them, how huge they can get, the universe
caving in, a star exploding, our earth,
it's surface green and arid yellow and frothy blue,

where decisions can be made by leaders
that affect the big things, so I, for safety sake,
come in closer. Sometimes it's just death we don't

want to think about and that we know so well
in such small detail, the death of our shining
country or of our smiling sister, and I remember

her standing in front of her apartment door,
wearing her new white winter coat, waving goodbye
for the last time and I wonder if I could have

said anything to change it and then I know that it's bigger
than that.

GIVING THANKS FOR THE TURKEY

We watch mother stick
the thermometer in the turkey's
browned flesh and wonder: are we well?
are we getting better?

We once had a brother who threw
the black cat, Whiskers, up high
into the air to see the look of
alarm and limbs akimbo and we try
not to imagine how his body
must have flown across the freeway
hit by an unseeing car at sixty,
his legs and arms doing their last strokes
through the air. No place is set for
him at the dinner table. Dad watches
the football game alone.

We once had a sister who made up words
and drank too much, the words rising
out of her, the liquor taking their place,
little left in her when a stranger came
to steal her final breath away.

On this day we are subdued and spit
the thanks out of our mouths,
a splintered bone, dangerous to us,
wanting to lodge in our throats. We say
aloud, *the pumpkin pie is good, the wild
rice superb*, and to ourselves, please,
let no one else be missing next year.

Giving Thanks for the Turkey

Let's start again. Let's give thanks for
ducks rising, lacy yarrow, window-paned ponds,
snow days, wood ticks, and glass jars full of agates.
Let's start at the other end of things,
where we see what has happened, where
the dog of understanding lies under
the table at our feet and waits for the turkey's neck.
We can begin by giving thanks for the turkey,
the bird of plenty, ugly and fierce in life,
comforting and delicious in death. We will
eat the light and dark meat of the turkey,
say, *it's done perfectly*, how could it be
any other way.